BRUCE ROGERS
DESIGNER OF BOOKS

LONDON : HUMPHREY MILFORD
OXFORD UNIVERSITY PRESS

BRUCE ROGERS

DESIGNER OF BOOKS

BY

FREDERIC WARDE

WITH A LIST OF THE BOOKS PRINTED UNDER

MR. ROGERS'S SUPERVISION

CAMBRIDGE

HARVARD UNIVERSITY PRESS

1925

NOTE

THIS monograph appeared originally in the fourth number of *The Fleuron*, and is here reprinted with a few alterations.

The list that follows the text comprises practically all the books designed by Mr. Rogers during the past thirty years which either possess literary value or are of special interest because of the manner of presentation. This latter consideration admits several items which can hardly be called books; but they may be of value to other students and practitioners of printing by reason of the typographical problems involved.

It has been difficult to determine the question of entire responsibility for many items; asterisks prefixed to the serial numbers indicate those books in which he has had the largest freedom and which have been made under his immediate direction.

The chronological arrangement of this hand-list and the abbreviated form of many of the titles will hardly commend it to bibliographers, but the consecutive numbering and the index at the end will, it is hoped, sufficiently take the place of an alphabetical arrangement.

BRUCE ROGERS

DESIGNER OF BOOKS

✡

NEARLY a decade has passed since Mr. Bruce Rogers last visited England, his position among the foremost living typographers already established within the circle of those who talk about printing. In the intervening years the coming of peace has widened this circle with extraordinary rapidity. Men's thoughts, tired of the clumsy businesses of death, have turned gratefully to those forms of Art where minute differences, fine details, may be handled with precision and made to seem important. None of the arts is more concerned with minutiæ than is book design. From the proportionate weight of the smallest type-face to the plan of the binding, there is no least detail which can be altered without altering the colour and feeling of the whole work; and typographic criticism, especially of the more speculative kind, is at its best and most fruitful upon some apparently microscopic point. Whether or not this fact may explain the growth of post-war interest in the study and collection of fine typography, the truth remains that general interest was never more lively, students never more admirably intent on present-day work. Collectors, newly started on the hazardous task of selecting modern examples, are learning to back their own judgment; but at first they find it best, like all other cautious connoisseurs, to 'play safe with the classics.'

Mr. Rogers, therefore, finds himself prematurely an old master, with a larger number of admirers than has followed a book designer, as such, for a long time. What fame he had before the war has increased with the number of the instructed; what influence his methods have had upon contemporaries — and it has been sharply traceable — has become far more important now that there are so many more printers aspiring to the level of his work.

Those who have played the largest part in making the thistle mark and the imprint 'B R' prominent in auction rooms and sales catalogues are amateurs of two kinds. There is the student of typography, who has found that each volume thus marked offers legitimate yet audacious points of comparison with some historical manner of printing, thus subtly challenging his learning and his taste. And there is the bibliophile, who finds the same fascination in a collection of Rogers imprints that he would find in the company of some-

2

one who could play faultlessly upon fifteen instruments; it is this type of admirer who dwells upon the range of style in the printer's work, as if his versatility were almost a freak of nature rather than the normal working of a mind nicely balanced between sympathy and intolerance.

Numerically this latter class makes up a large proportion of Mr. Rogers's public, so we are not surprised to find his reputation resting in the main upon certain books which have become classics in the sort of typography we call 'allusive,' in that the design alludes to, or even quotes from, some historic style. Given a piece of literature, preferably dating from a past age, the object of the graceful game is to create for it the most appropriate possible setting without falling into any archaisms which would distract the reader. Of such are most of the Riverside Press Editions designed by Mr. Rogers, as well as many of the more elaborate limited editions that he has produced since their time. In fact, the sort of book which he has been asked to print has been, in almost every case where great pains could be taken with the production, one where a certain powdering of antiquity was plainly called for. Given a book on *Franklin and his Press at Passy*, the designer can only accept one historical manner of type arrangement and set himself to surpass his models

3

in adroitness, if the book is to have any distinction beyond that of sound craftsmanship. To give it a dress which Franklin would have thought unpleasant or strange would be officious.

But to take Mr. Rogers purely on the valuation of the student and amateur is to rate him as little more than a designer of historical costumes for books, and to ignore the twofold contribution which he has made to fine modern book-making. Certain qualities of his work are important to the practising printer quite apart from any supposed relation between an author and a type-face. There is a third class of 'B R' collectors, the men who are concerned in the possible evolution of a modern style through their own efforts. Such persons will want to own the Grolier Club *Pierrot of the Minute*, because they alone, from practical knowledge of the craft, can appreciate the mechanical deftness of the work. If they cannot explain the casual felicity of the whole book, they can at least single out each evidence of technical mastery. In a time of impetuous and not over-meticulous artisanship the mere sight of such a piece of work has an effect at once humbling and provocative to those who are capable of analysing its merits. Unfortunately, the *Pierrot* is found only on the shelves of three hundred bibliophiles who subscribed for it. However few are the printers who affect in any way the general level of typographic style, few of these few have been able to examine this book in detail. Hence such museum-pieces are of less direct importance than they otherwise would be.

There has been, however, a new direction in Mr. Rogers's work in the last few years which has given his contemporaries at least a hint toward a novel and individual manner. He has been conducting experiments, quite as often upon trade editions as on limited reprints; experiments whose object, quite apart from any 'period' considerations, is to produce new effects from new combinations of actual working material that any printer may possess. The importance of these essays, and the probable direction of Mr. Rogers's future development, may be more clearly gauged after an examination of his past interests and work.

Those who know him find that his creative curiosity — what may be called his manual wit in attacking technical problems — is not confined to the making of books and broadsides. The same ingenuity distinguishes his *ex-libris*, which are so little known, the tooled bindings on which he experiments, and, perhaps most characteristically, an occasional ship-model which he builds and rigs with scrupulous cunning. This nimbleness of hand and judgment is, indeed, common to artificers of all times and countries. Perhaps the only trait in Mr. Rogers which can be called definitely national is that twist of American temperament which is somewhat inconveniently termed humour. If this dry and restless mockery be spelled 'humor' in its native fashion, there may be less danger of confusing it with the more complacent European variety. It is a sort of critical whimsy: there is little cheer in it and no cheerio, but there is instead a robust and sardonic inventiveness which will always freshen and goad on the creative worker. It is at its salt-and-bitterest in New England; but in transit to the Middle West it has become mellower, the scepticism combines with a certain sympathy, and the combination may produce a Mark Twain or a Booth Tarkington. Especially, in that section, does the state of Indiana seem to have a stimulating mental climate. In any group of American great or well-known will be found an amazing, an incredible proportion of Indiana-born. Mr. Rogers qualified for this distinction in the village of Linnwood, which is now a part of the city of Lafayette. Some of his ancestors had come overland as pioneers from Virginia in the hazardous days of the Conestoga wagon; they were sportsmen and wilderness-breakers, and, like their descendant, they had no great affection for cities and no particular

6

enthusiasm for continuous social contact with their fellow-men. From his father Mr. Rogers had learned to develop an inherited talent for drawing and penmanship, so that when he entered Purdue University at sixteen, he was prepared to make the most of advanced courses in draughting and decorative design. He decided to become an illustrator, and in order to gain experience, he worked on the staff of several undergraduate publications. Even at that time the arrangement of type on paper was of strong interest to him. He tells of bringing home from the library several volumes of the works of the earliest and most interminable American novelist, Charles Brockden Brown, simply because the printing and binding of that particular edition seemed so pleasant to him. He would open and handle the books, turning the crisp leaves; had the text been less turgid, he might even have read it, as a final tribute to typographic merit.

In the year of his graduation, 1890, plans were already being made in England for the establishment of the Kelmscott Press. William Morris, a giant with a plough, was turning up fresh soil under the dry technicalities of printing. All definitions had to be reconsidered, and what is more important, reworded in such simple and vigorous terms that the general public found itself able to

7

argue about the essentials of good printing and to use this new vocabulary to rebuke feeble work. When the young Rogers became an illustrator on the *Indianapolis News* he had heard nothing of this subversive movement, but he had realised, however, that illustration was interesting to him only as a means of beautifying books. The rapid-fire sketching demanded in newspaper work was distasteful to him, and after a season of it he resigned and went back to Lafayette, to spend some time in landscape painting. This avocation was to provide him throughout his life with a record of the various outdoor aspects of countries where he has lived, and in his paintings he has put down for his own delight the contours of hills and sea-shore, where he feels most at home.

Upon his return to Indianapolis as a general draughtsman, he made the acquaintance of Mr. J. M. Bowles, the founder of a quarterly, *Modern Art*, which was one of the first American reflections of the new Arts and Crafts movement. Mr. Bowles had some of the Kelmscott books and showed them to Mr. Rogers, to whom they came as a revelation. He has said that upon seeing Morris's printing, his whole interest in book-production became rationalised and intensified. He abandoned the prevalent idea that a book could be made beautiful through the work of an illustrator alone, and determined instead to use that curiosity he had always felt as to type and paper, toward a study of the physical form of printed books. Naturally anything which could so thoroughly satisfy his eyes as *Poems by the Way* would have an effect, however transitory, on his efforts. While still in college he had lettered one or two title-pages for Thomas B. Mosher, and in 1895 the name 'Bruce Rogers' appears for the first time in a colophon, as designer of a few insignificant decorations for one of Mr. Mosher's publications — A. E.'s *Homeward Songs by the Way*. A better opportunity to express his new opinions came when Mr. Bowles undertook the production of R. B. Gruelle's *Notes on the Walters Collection*. In this catalogue, also published in 1895, in addition to designing the title-page, initials and chapter headings, he had a hand in proportioning the page and margins. Set in that bold and humourless type known as 'Bookman,' the page preserves its 'unity' (the word was a battle-cry) in the decorations, which were stolid in themselves, but bold and simple enough to support the colour of the whole.

Modern Art gained popularity and lost money until it was subsidised by a wealthy firm of 'art publishers,' L. Prang and Company, of Boston, who in 1895 persuaded Mr. Bowles to edit the

in its more brilliant and subtle forms was, after all, a new thing then. One suspects Mr. Updike, if not of having invented it, at least of having found it in the nursery and left it in the drawing-room. There can be no doubt of the influence of the Merrymount Press and its brilliant director upon Mr. Rogers, not only during the nineties while Mr. Updike was engaged in his more daring experiments, but also later, while he was issuing as a publisher his *Humanists' Library* for much the same type of reader as that which supported the special book-making at the Riverside Press. The advice and encouragement that Mr. Updike always offers to the student were particularly valued by his new friend in Cambridge.

The Riverside Press Editions probably owed their immediate and remarkable effect on a section of the reading public to the policy of 'individual treatment' mentioned above. Book-lovers, their tastes stimulated by the founders of semi-private presses in England, had begun to weary of the succession of vellum-bound quartos in one home-made type which seemed to be the usual product of those presses. These new editions did not form a 'set,' or even, through any physical similarity, a series. It was partly the unexpectedness of each new format that from the very first exhausted many of the editions before the date of publication. The work of the Department of Special Book-making has been reviewed by several hands in considerable detail. Mr. Alfred W. Pollard in particular has given us so discriminating an account of this period in the designer's activity that later comment, except for the purpose of summary, is hardly necessary. Several items should be mentioned here as being of special importance. The second book to appear in 1900 was the *Rubáiyát of Omar Khayyám*, a work which, like *Aucassin and Nicolette*, had been issued from nearly every private press that took itself seriously. This particular edition marks the first use after many years of the 'Brimmer' type, a transitional face of great vigour (listed on the records of the Bruce Type Foundry as a private face, cut at an unknown date by one Simpson), an obsolete fount of which Mr. Rogers had discovered in the obscurity of the composing room at Riverside. The American Type Founders were commissioned to make new matrices and cast the type specially for the Press, and to cut special swash capitals for the italic after Mr. Rogers's design. Brimmer was used in at least one book a year during the time that Mr. Rogers was at Cambridge.

But the Press was not devoting itself entirely to the production of slender octavos. The project of printing the *Essays* of Montaigne in three folio volumes had been considered from the first, and in view of the imposing scale of the work it was decided to have a special type cut for it which would have boldness and distinction in as large a size as sixteen-point. Mr. Rogers went back, in the healthy fashion of the time, to the Jenson letter and drew from it a design eminently fitted to its purpose. Montaigne type has been used (not by Mr. Rogers) upon coated paper, which makes it look pedantic and uninteresting; properly inked and printed, it is both graceful and dignified. A trial fount was used in 1902 to print Sir Walter Raleigh's account of *The Last Fight of the Revenge at Sea*. This was the first Riverside book printed on a hand-press; it should, however, be noted that the old Adams platen presses used for printing many of the other volumes approximated the motion and results of the hand-press. A woodcut after Howard Pyle on the title-page of the Raleigh showed for the first time the work of an illustrator coming to the aid of the typographer; in this case the vigorous renaissance woodcut border which surrounds it, and the massed weight of the Montaigne type on the text page support it effectively. But in the edition of Spenser's *Prothalamion and Epithalamion*, printed in the same year, the book is only weakened by the reproduction in photogravure of the vignettes

14

and illustrations designed by the mural painter, Mr. Edwin H. Blashfield.

Experiments were continued with the Montaigne fount until the last volume of the *Essays* had been set in 1904. He was not entirely pleased with the face as it appeared, even after many alterations. In a way, the punch-cutter had done his work too well; Mr. Rogers decided that there had been too much 'improvement' over the original, and he resolved to return to Jenson at some later time for a more direct inspiration. Meanwhile the Montaigne was used in an edition of Boccaccio's *Life of Dante*, a simple and stately book, and later on, in 1908, appeared in the duodecimo *Banquet* of Plato. In spite of the fact that the type was cut for use on a large page, its use in the short lines and small pages of the latter book is unexpectedly pleasing. The book cannot, perhaps, be read as fast as if the line were longer or the type smaller; but to put this forward as an objection is to imply that the reader is capable of following Plato's reasoning as swiftly as his eyes can skim the line. Its value in this particular edition lies not in the fact that it can be read rapidly, but in the fact that it presents the text in a manner just sufficiently unusual and impressive to command and direct attention. It is used here without decoration.

The first book done at Riverside in black-letter was *The History of Oliver and Arthur* (1903), in which Priory Text, and woodcuts reproduced in facsimile from an early edition, combine to give a studiously historic appearance to the work. Far more sprightly is the use of a French *lettre bâtarde* in Chaucer's *Parlement of Foules*, which appeared soon after, and in *The Song of Roland* (1906), which is now one of the most sought-for of all the Riverside Press Editions. In this last book the decorations were printed from line blocks and coloured by hand in imitation of a series of stained-glass roundels in the Cathedral of Chartres — a touch of romanticism which pleases the collector as much as do the marginal notes, which are printed in *civilité* and look surprisingly like the faded holograph comments of some sixteenth-century owner. These three books constitute the only Riverside experiments in mediævalism, and none can be said to be as grateful to the eyes as the three books in the classic style which were also appearing during this time. These latter were set in Brimmer, the first and third being in italic. The second one, Plutarch's *Consolatorie Letter or Discourse*, has for its only decoration a photogravure, on the title-page, of an Attic stele. The *Georgics* of Virgil and the *Idylls* of Theocritus are accompanied by wood-engravings by Mr. M. Lamont

Brown, some after drawings by Mr. Rogers and some after antique gems and seals. In the Theocritus the decorations combine happily with the type. Mr. Rogers's own leanings toward the art-forms of ancient Greece have always given warmth and sympathy to his essays in the classic manner; indeed, it may be possible that his understanding of renaissance typography is due to the fact that he, too, is prepossessed with pagan culture.

The year 1909, while not as productive as earlier years, was marked by the appearance of two noteworthy books, one presenting the most difficult of tasks, and the other, in appearance at least, of the most candid simplicity. The first was Mr. G. B. Ives's translation of Bernard's *Geofroy Tory*, in which many examples of Tory's work had to be shown. In order to do justice to the original woodcuts, each one was photographed and re-touched by Mr. Rogers with exquisite care, to eliminate the faults of over-inking, poor press-work, or damage to the block that were present in the original impression. Borders thus restored to the state in which Tory would have wished them to appear could no longer be used in conjunction with the undistinguished and over-inked roman types which they had originally surrounded, so, as a courageous move, it was decided to print the actual text of the book inside the borders whenever they occurred. Thus the question of an appropriate type became paramount. As a result came Riverside Caslon, a type which Mr. Rogers remodelled from fourteen-point foundry lowercase Caslon and twelve-point capitals, to suit his needs. An extraordinary amount of ingenuity with a graver went into the actual remodelling of each character in the fount; the original types were made richer in colour by rubbing down the printing surfaces, they were made to set closer together, and after innumerable experiments the resulting characters were employed to make electrotyped matrices. The matrices, in turn, were fitted to a monotype casting machine, sorts were produced at the Press, and the book was set by hand. The result is curiously unlike Caslon, and in the close setting and general weight a most satisfactory approximation of the types of Tory's time. The other book that appeared in this year is *The Compleat Angler*, in which this compact type again is used. Few sextodecimos are more *aimable* than this, one of Mr. Rogers's favourite books.

Tory's woodcut borders (not yet staled by custom) were never more gracefully used than in the *Ecclesiastes*, printed in 1911, a book in which Mr. Rogers heroically restrained himself from adding to the sum of famous biblical misprints. The temptation to make the copy read 'of the making of many books there is *an* end' is understandable when we realize that this was the last of those fifty editions which, printed under such happy circumstances, will always be his most imposing monument. The Houghton Mifflin Company had by this time somewhat altered its policy of leisurely idealism, and Mr. Rogers on his part had begun to hope for a more independent career. Business relations were, therefore, ended in 1912, and Mr. Rogers spent a summer in travel abroad, writing, on the passage over, a brief review of the work of some American printers — including his own — for the printing number of the London *Times*, and again visiting Mr. Emery Walker.

Upon returning to America, Mr. Rogers became a free lance in his profession. 'I'd like to be a tramp printer,' he said; and indeed those who know him and his love of the open country understand the project, which he still cherishes, of going into rural retreat at some converted mill, with only a few types, a portable press, and a sketching-pad. At that time, however, the ears of publishers were not yet tuned to the golden clink of fine printing, and commissions were few. He went to New York and maintained himself there for three grey years by commercial work. Of the four signed books which belong to this period, two were commissioned by societies of wealthy book-lovers, one by a museum, and the fourth was privately printed for an amateur. As a result, the printing has that precious and antiquarian look that so well pleases the cultured subscriber to editions, who likes to recognize and beam upon an adroit historical mannerism. *Franklin and his Press at Passy* (New York, The Grolier Club, 1914) has been taken as one of the finest examples we have of reminiscent printing. There is no trickery in it, — Mr. Rogers has never 'faked' an effect with battered type and a heavy impression, — yet the simple embellishments which he drew and the Brimmer and Oxford types which are so appropriate for the time in which Franklin moved, both take every possible advantage of history.

Even before 1914, the Metropolitan Museum of Art in New York City had begun, under the direction of Mr. H. W. Kent, its Secretary, a series of experiments which were to associate it very intimately with the progress of American typography. Mr. Kent's Museum Press is the despair of collectors; for though its output of broadsides, memorials, and greetings is constant and of superlative quality, the number of impressions of each item ranges from two or three to a very few. Even beyond his own work, however, Mr. Kent's influence upon contemporary taste in his country has been noteworthy, for as President of the Grolier Club and a factor in other *sociétés d'encouragement* he has been in a position to support his keen judgement with substantial commissions. Mr. Rogers had already been associated with the Museum's new activity; in 1912 he designed for it *Les Points de France*, a book on laces, and during the next year he produced, in association with Mr. Kent, several monumental testimonials and posters. Meanwhile Mr. Rogers's second thought about Jenson's type had reached the point of completion on paper, and the design was ready to be cut. Mr. Kent, upon seeing it, hailed it as a masterpiece; the Museum purchased the right to use the capital letters, had them cut in several sizes, and has ever since reserved this famous type for the occasional works where it may be shown to perfect advantage. An effective use of this letter, 'Centaur,' is in the case labels, some of which are printed in gold upon black, for the Museum's collection of armour.

Meanwhile the international fame of the Riverside books was still increasing. In 1915 Mr. Pollard read before the Bibliographical Society an estimate of Mr. Rogers's work.[1] It was the first

1. *The Work of Bruce Rogers, Printer*, by Alfred W. Pollard. A Paper read before the Bibliographical Society, October 18, 1915. Summary printed in the Society's 'News-Sheet,' London, November, 1915. Printed (somewhat abridged) in the Society's 'Transactions,' London, 1919. Separate pamphlet reprinted from the 'Transactions,' by Blades, East & Blades, London, 1919.

time that a living printer had been thus honoured, and the praise, coming from so high an authority, had considerable effect on Athenians abroad and in the United States who had not before heard of this new thing. In June, 1916, an exhibition of Mr. Rogers's books, arranged by Mr. John Cotton Dana at the Newark (New Jersey) Public Library, brought together for the first time practically all the books and most of the broadsides which he had designed at Cambridge and elsewhere. The Carteret Club of that city simultaneously issued a catalogue, with an earlier essay of Mr. Pollard's on *Modern Fine Printing in England and Mr. Bruce Rogers.*

The year 1915 had brought more opportunity. He produced *An Account of Strawberry Hill Catalogues* for Mr. Percival Merritt, as well as a memorial of *Luther S. Livingston.* At that time Mr. Carl P. Rollins, now Printer to Yale University, was conducting his lively and distinguished Montague Press at the Dyke Mill in the village of Montague, Massachusetts. In spite of the rustic scenery around the Dyke Mill, this was a commercial and not a private press. Its owner, however, could and did offer Mr. Rogers a chance to collaborate with him in typographic experiments of the most idealistic kind.

One result of Mr. Rogers's visit to Montague

was the book which gave its name to his new type: *The Centaur*, by Maurice de Guérin, translated by Mr. Ives. One hundred and thirty-five copies were printed, of which some sixty were presented by the printer to friends. The first use of the Centaur type in book work was a revelation of the possibilities of the design. It was produced by drawing or writing over enlarged photographs of the Jenson roman; but to say only this would be to mislead the reader, unless he is aware of the infinite discretion and observation needed for such a task. Mr. Rogers realized that the photographic enlargements of the old type face must be neither oversize nor undersize in proportion to the actual size of the type, because the effect of his drawing of the letters would show in the final form either over-modelling on too large a scale or perhaps under-modelling on too small a scale. The recutting of an old type face from the printed form of the letter requires the utmost pains and care in order to avoid a tawdry result. The surplus of ink that had accumulated on the type must be considered, the probable wear on the printing surfaces by previous printings must be calculated, the amount of impression used in printing the type must be observed, and whether the paper was too wet or too dry; withal, what effect one or all of these

23

factors have had upon the true outline of the characters. All or any of these may conspire to deflect the intended result. To see even beyond these accidents into the essential consistency of the face and find in it warrant to change minor details (such as eliminating the inner 'slab' serifs of the capital M) is work requiring almost clairvoyant ability. In the fourteen-point size of Centaur, several letters have been revised even up to the present time. The curve and end of the tail of the lower-case 'y' have been altered; the lower-case 'e' with a horizontal stroke, forming the lower part of the eye, has been added as an alternate letter with the other 'e' with the oblique stroke. In the present use of Centaur, diamond-shaped points (periods, semicolons, colons, etc.) have been substituted for the round ones. The designer or punch-cutter must not aim, however, to perfect the outline in every way. The Montaigne type, perhaps because it was cut only in a large size, errs in this direction. Centaur, especially in the fourteen-point size used in *The Centaur*, looks almost diffident after the bold strict curves of the Doves or Distel romans, but it is for that reason of greater charm to the reader. Used as it was in that book, with a renaissance headband and initial redrawn in precisely the right colour, the effect was beyond praise. The book was

24

accepted by many as the masterpiece of modern printing.

Upon his return to New York from Montague, Mr. Rogers became an occasional aid to the Museum Press. Among his friends abroad with whom he had corresponded regularly was Mr. Emery Walker, who had earlier withdrawn from partnership in the Doves Press, and now was considering founding a press of his own at Hammersmith. The ideals of the two men were so essentially alike that it was natural for Mr. Walker to invite his friend to share in the project, and for Mr. Rogers to look forward to work in the country which had always afforded him such a friendly welcome. It became known that he would sail for England at the end of 1916. The news was received somewhat ruefully by the group who had come to realize what an effect his work would have upon contemporary printing, now that it was being exhibited and reproduced in facsimile so frequently. The essential of American style, if there be any such style, is surely eclecticism: no local tradition, especially in type-usage, is strong enough to make the use of a 'foreign' type seem precious, or an ancient decoration seem uncouth. And now the chief prophet of eclecticism was to depart for a Caslon-ridden country, leaving the future of fine printing

25

in America almost entirely in the capable hands of Mr. Updike.

No less auspicious time could have been chosen for the establishment of the Mall Press than the early months of 1917. Mr. Rogers's first book there was a commission from the Grolier Club to reprint a translation of that part of Albrecht Dürer's *Geometriæ*, which deals with the design of letters for inscriptions. The edition of 318 copies of *On the Just Shaping of Letters* was completed by August, under the most trying conditions. Almost from the beginning there were no trained workmen available. Though Mr. Rogers had only a theoretical knowledge of the actual operations of printing, the thoroughness of this knowledge now came to his aid. He made ready forms with his own hands, and put the sheets through the press. In spite of these difficulties and the additional trouble of printing three copies upon refractory vellum, the book is distinguished not only for its design and for the magnificently drawn Dürer-esque title-page, but for the admirable inking and impression which brings out the full beauty of the Centaur type. *On the Just Shaping of Letters* eventually brought such a fabulous price in the auction rooms that designers began, not unreasonably, to begrudge to the wealthy collector this series of noble letters. The practical ones have, however, been appeased with Mr. Rogers's later impression of *The Construction of Roman Letters by Albrecht Dürer* (Dunster House, Cambridge, 1924), in which the blocks alone are printed on a 16mo page of pale grey paper, which softens the blackness of the broad inked surfaces.

The Dürer book was the only one printed by Mr. Rogers at the Mall Press. On its completion he was invited by the Syndics of the Cambridge University Press to assume the position of Printing Adviser to the Press under the direction of Mr. J. B. Peace, who was Printer to the University until his death in 1923. The work and the surroundings proved congenial, and the next twenty-one months were occupied in quiet experimentation and research at Cambridge. During this time the Centaur fount, which had followed its designer abroad, was used only in small privately printed books and greetings, such as a quarto edition of Dr. M. R. James's *Address* before the Tipperary Club (1918), and *Spare your Good* (1919). The possible uses of printers' 'flowers,' or units of type ornament, some of which he had recut and occasionally employed at Riverside, again began to arouse his curiosity. Available material seemed too elaborate and refined, and he resorted to a simple expedient to re-create the bold, traditional arabesque forms which were evolved by type-founders before the end of the sixteenth century. A drawing of a complete arabesque pattern from an old book was photographically enlarged, and a line cut made of the enlargement; from this cut several proofs were taken. In order to achieve that ingenious variety which is the never-failing interest of such forms, the printed proofs were cut up into their simplest component units, and these units were shifted and rearranged to form different patterns. When a particular combination had been invented, it was carefully pasted together, and from this was made the reduced zinc block which was to be employed in the actual printing. It was frankly a hurried makeshift, but the effect was happy, the combinations (best seen in the privately printed poem *On Friendship*, 1918) were fresh and interesting, and the later result of the revival was, as we shall see, practically a new development in modern decorative printing.

Another essay in designing was the result of a commission, from the Pelican Press in London, for a poster letter. Mr. Rogers drew a complete alphabet of roman capitals and lower-case letters and figures. These designs were rendered on wood, and not as carefully as one could wish; at that time, however, skilled mechanics were not available for such work. To-day these letters are used frequently for posters which may be seen in almost any London underground station, and it is hoped by those who have seen the original drawings that one day all the letters will be recut competently.

A new type-acquaintance was made in an old-style face which probably originated with Fry, and now is known as Georgian. This type was used in some of the minor pieces of printing, such as the 16mo edition of *Address at Unveiling the Roll of Honour* (Cambridge, 1918) and *A Collection of Books about Cats* (Cambridge, 1918); and the care and attention given by Mr. Rogers to the spacing between words and leading between lines shows plainly what understanding of these matters can accomplish. Of greater importance than these small items was the main work which he had to do: to modify and reform the typography of the University publications, to suggest standards of spacing and arrangement, to work out proportions of page and margin in books which could not possibly be seen through the presses with that scrupulous attention which every book receives that carries his mark. He had to arrange for the destruction of much old and bad type, and he had to search the ancient institution for material worthy of being revived. His work with trade editions drew upon his practical ingenuities just as it had at the Riverside Press, and the stricter conditions of economical production may perhaps have proved a contrast and a spur after five years of creating limited numbers of perfect copies. Cambridge typography rose almost at once to a high level of excellence, which it maintains to-day. Only one or two of the present workmen knew him. The style of the books now printed there can hardly be attributed to the lingering influence of his preferences in spacing or the use of types. It was rather by creating an audience of discriminating critics among those scholars whom such an institution serves that Mr. Rogers helped to give the Press its present standing, if not its present style.

For nine months after the Armistice he continued to work at Cambridge. Post-war depression, however, delayed the programme of finely printed editions which had most interested him. His former associates in America, supported by the wave of prosperity which was then sweeping over the country, found themselves able to experiment, to spend money in realising cherished theories; indeed, those designers who had fallen from respectable book-work into advertising were finding it difficult to spend enough money to mitigate their clients' income taxes. This enhanced opportunity, as well as ill health and the need for the more kindly climate of his own country, may have brought Mr. Rogers's visit to an earlier close than it would otherwise have had. He parted with the keenest regret from the town and countryside which he had explored so minutely, and from those friends in the University who, like any unsociable man's friends, had been diffidently chosen and warmly cherished.

For several years he had, on occasion, coöperated with the Harvard University Press in Cambridge, Massachusetts, as critic of some of its productions. Upon his return to America, Harvard conferred on him the official position, which he still holds, of Printing Adviser to the Press. The Harvard University Press is a well-equipped institution, blessed above its fellows with officers and supporters who have enthusiasms about printing. It has also had the good fortune to collaborate with Mr. Updike and with such learned bibliographers as Mr. George Parker Winship. In consequence, the standard of execution is high, and Mr. Rogers has not found it necessary to go into the more elementary details in planning a format, a thing which he could not spare time for in unsigned work. When a press reaches a certain point of technical excellence and has come to be known for a definite style of its own, it is often in the greatest need of creative suggestions from an outsider, to prevent staleness in treatment. When it can avail itself of the curiosity and ingenuity of a Bruce Rogers, whose chosen motto is *Vivificat vitam varietas*, one may expect those almost flawless books which are the perfection of trade editions. It was, then, at Harvard that Mr. Rogers reaccustomed himself to America and surveyed the field of opportunity.

Among the New York printing houses that of William Edwin Rudge was attracting considerable attention through the ability of its proprietor to give his work magnificence without making it look foolish. Mr. Rudge was aided by the current demand for magnificence; but so were a score of nearsighted contemporaries whom the impending panic was to throw into such embarrassment. What Mr. Rudge possessed in addition was a sincere ambition to do book printing of permanent quality. Mr. Rogers was accordingly offered the task of designing the more particular pieces of printing that the Rudge establishment was to produce. He agreed, and again moved to New York, where Mr. Rudge was just completing the remodelling of his newly acquired building at Mount Vernon. One of the first results of this association was the booklet *The Night before Christmas*, sent out as a holiday greeting in 1920. Printed in that dashing italic of mysterious origin, eighteen-point Original Old Style, the book's waggish air promised much to lovers of light-hearted printing.

In spite of his frequent use of post-Caslon types in the past, and his paraphrase of the fifteenth-century letter of Jenson, Mr. Rogers was still expected to perform his best and happiest work in the manner of the French sixteenth century; indeed, his treatment of Centaur has always been such as to bring out the qualities in Jenson's original that seem most removed from the buxom printing of the early Renaissance, and nearest related to the italianate French productions of half a century later. Thus the most exigent student of 'periods' could not object to the Estienne heading and initial which, in *The Centaur*, are used with a type which is in essence Jenson's. It is a mooted question of the nuances of colour; Cloister Old Style, which follows Jenson more literally from impressions of his type in damp paper, is altogether too heavy in colour to be supported by the delicate decoration of a later style. As one most competent to revive the traditions of sixteenth-century masters, Mr. Rogers was looked to with great interest, upon its completion in 1920, for his first use of the new Garamond series which the American Type Founders Company had brought out at the suggestion of Mr. Henry L. Bullen. The full range of sizes had been cut in time for the semi-centennial of the Metropolitan Museum in 1920, when it was most effectively used in various pieces of occasional printing by the Museum Press. Those who had expected a piece of 'period' work were surprised in that year by the appearance of *The Journal of Madam Knight*, a reprinted account of the wanderings of a sprightly eighteenth-century lady through colonial New England; nothing could be more definitely removed from dignified sixteenth-century printing than this calico-covered volume with jolly lineblocks in Papillon's manner, and an amusing map. Yet the sharp, whimsical character of Garamond has seldom been turned to better account. Had the book been printed in Caslon, it would have been simply imitative and perhaps consciously 'quaint.' If, indeed, we grant the obvious fact that the choice of type gives the essential flavour to a piece of printing, it may be contended that Mr. Rogers has never designed a book which can be called, *in toto*, 'sixteenth-century,' that is, one in which all the typographic elements are inspired by the best work of that single epoch. Even the new *Champ Fleury*, which follows the general arrangement of the first edition as closely and gravely as a good angel might follow a toper, is set in Centaur. Those volumes, on the other hand, which do make use of the only sixteenth-century

34

face available in America, are either given decoration not strictly conforming to the supposed date of the type, like *Madam Knight*, or are without any definite reminiscence, purely original things, like *Night and Moonlight*. The exceptional case of the Garamont number of *Monotype* may be counted more as a type specimen than as an example of book-making. That Mr. Rogers enjoys his widest reputation as a worker in the sixteenth-century style must, then, arise from his prepossessions in the past for certain uses of woodcut ornament, rather than from any attempt on his part to imitate as closely as possible the masterpieces of the time of the Estiennes. The ease and sympathy of his handling of Renaissance styles enables him to take liberties which he has not allowed himself, at least in some of his earlier work, with modern faces. The conscious effort toward a 'period' is far more evident in *Paul et Virginie* than in the *Ronsard*, for example; the former, as Mr. Pollard says, 'might have come straight from Didot's workship' — a dubious compliment akin to saying that a certain coin might have come straight from the mint. Yet in spite of this and of other *tours de force* in post-Caslon or modern types, Mr. Rogers is not generally assigned, as Mr. Updike has somewhat too hastily been, to the last quarter of the eighteenth and the first

quarter of the nineteenth centuries for his resources and inspirations, but to the earlier epoch;
although, now that he has almost entirely abandoned the use of drawn or woodcut ornament,
this idea may have to be reconsidered.

Among the first Rogers imprints executed at
Mr. Rudge's establishment were those published
by Dunster House, a bookshop in Cambridge,
Massachusetts. They include the lean and somewhat stark-looking volume, *The Red Path and
The Wounded Bird*, two poems by John Freeman
(Cambridge, 1921), and a catalogue of *Books from
the Library of the Late John Williams White*, issued in the same year. In the next year Dunster
House also published *Priapus and the Pool*, a collection of poems by Conrad Aiken. In this, as in
the Freeman book, Mr. Rogers had the problem
of presenting a modern work in which any typographic borrowing from antiquity would have
been, in the stricter sense, impertinent. *Priapus
and the Pool* uses no counter-attraction of line-cut
decoration or unaccustomed type-setting against
the beauty of Mr. Aiken's poetry. The type is
Original Old Style (Linotype), the size and arrangement of the page are admirably suited to the
uneven lines of verse. Two thread-like bands of
lozenge rule on the title-page, together with the
Dunster House monogram, constitute all of the

decoration. For no too-obvious reason, the book is a completely delightful thing. Another book which is effective through simplicity is *Night and Moonlight*, by Henry D. Thoreau (New York, Hubert R. Brown, 1921). According to the advertisement with which Mr. Rogers announced this book, it was to be the first of a series (of which Dürer's Roman Letters was to be the second): 'In my intervals of leisure I intend to print several little books whose subjects will be my own choice. The selection will conform to no premeditated plan and the list will probably be as varied in content as in typography. The first of these publications, a reprint of Thoreau's *Night and Moonlight*, is now ready for distribution. First published in the *Atlantic Monthly* in 1863, it was later included in the *Miscellanies*, but has never before been issued in separate form, so far as I know. Though one of the shortest, it is perhaps the most poetic of Thoreau's studies of landscape. He definitely intended to give it that quality, aiming, as he himself says, "to add to the domain of poetry"; and, in turn, I have endeavoured to make it an addition to the poetic side of book-making.'

The 'blonde' effect of *Night and Moonlight* is due in part to the use on the title-page of Goudy Open capitals and to the little crescent-moon brackets that surround the page-numbers. These

37

brackets were made from open-face capital O's, which were cut in half. The first page contains a woodcut in colours by Florence Wyman Ivins. The type is foundry Garamond, which was also used in the same year for a privately printed edition of Increase Mather's *Several Reasons*, a book which employed some of the line-blocks of arabesque flowers that had been used in England.

Mr. Rogers's interest in Garamond as a book face waned while this latter book was in progress, but the possibilities of printers' flowers appealed to him as never before. Drawing for reproduction with type he had always found difficult, and however effective the final result might be, he seldom was satisfied with it. Units of type ornament, on the other hand, are not only homogeneous with printing, but offer a range of combinations which, in the simpler forms, is almost endless. In the spring of 1921 he was one of the six printers invited by the Grolier Club each to produce a book of his own choice in his own way. The invitation came in good season, for a rush of more or less perfunctory work had settled upon him at Mount Vernon, and he was becoming irked and discouraged at his inability to spend enough time and pains on a few important things. His choice of material was Ernest Dowson's *Pierrot of the Minute*, a work which is closely associated in the minds of

Dowson readers with the illustrations of Aubrey Beardsley. Instead of again using these, he embowered the text in a combination of eighteenth-century ornaments. The poem is an echo of an artificial age by one who delighted in verbal artifice, and the Rogers edition, with its fragile garlands and moons printed in a soft rose-red, is a triumph of whimsical humour over the mechanics of type-setting. Mr. Kent owns a collection of progressive trial pages and proofs of the great number of combinations which were set up and discarded before the final result was obtained. The Deberny types, as well as the ornaments cut in imitation of Fournier's, had been imported from France. The *Pierrot* was ready for the press by the spring of 1922, but the choice of paper delayed publication.

Meanwhile Mr. Rogers had undertaken to design several books in a variety of modern types, which offer a sharp contrast, in their crisp severity, to the old-style fantasy of the *Pierrot*. It could not be called reaction from decoration, for Gallatin's *American Water-Colourists* (printed in Bodoni) has a title-page cleverly furbished with parentheses grouped as ornaments, while *The Presbyterian Child*, which appeared in the next year and is, perhaps, the most distinguished of his books in Scotch roman, is given an almost architectonic title-page by the use made of small dart motives. It was rather that these books, like almost all American editions, had to be set on composing machines, and the Monotype Scotch was the only face besides the perennial Caslon which seemed to offer possibilities. A new development by the Lanston Monotype Company, however, widened the field of choice, and was the occasion of Mr. Rogers's designing a type specimen which has hardly a peer for ingenuity: the 'Garamont issue' (Spring, 1923) of the periodical *Monotype*, in which appears the first official showing of the new type face adapted by Mr. Goudy from the design of the *caractères de l'Université* of the French National Printing Office. Mr. Rogers could find no ornaments of appropriate character for this face, which has a somewhat sharper appearance than the foundry version. Even had he wished to, he could hardly have drawn special decorations for a type specimen. Instead, he retouched and somewhat refined the drawings of 'flowers' which he had brought back from England, and had matrices engraved from these. The resulting type-ornaments may safely be called the most successful adaptation of traditional printers' motives that exists to-day. They were used in the Garamont number in a profusion of arrangements. The whole pamphlet seems to have been done in high spirits, and the designer breaks into a chuckle in the colophon:

'It only remains to add that, as an authority once said I was "still to be reckoned a limited edition man," I must bear out his classification, and incidentally give this note the characteristic colophonic flavor, by stating that this issue of *Monotype*, printed from type that will be destroyed (not distributed) after printing, is limited to 20,000 copies.'

In sober fact, the designer had been working for some time on a kind of book which was far removed from the preciousness we associate with limited editions. His name, it is true, has never been put upon an edition which could be allowed to go through the presses without his instant supervision; but this is mainly a guaranty against the depredations of long runs and mass-production methods. For example, in 1923 the Harvard University Press issued a limited edition of *Wordsworth in a New Light*, which was signed by him, and a trade edition on ordinary paper, cloth bound; the latter is somewhat smaller in size, but has the same typographical design and is in itself a thoroughly attractive piece of printing. Another Harvard book of his planning was Houston's *Doctor Johnson* (1924), which is so straightforward in its design that the average reader does not feel himself confronted with any mystery of fine typography, but finds instead a clear and inviting page, presumably full of the author's ideas. The lover of paintings is no longer allowed to ask that every picture tell a story, but the reader can and must ask typography to tell the author's story, without any talk of print for print's sake. It is unfortunate that this notion seems to be confined, among printers, to the humblest unenlightened on the one hand and to the rare virtuosi on the other, and that the otherwise ambitious do not regard it. Mr. Rogers has recently designed two books for Alfred A. Knopf, New York — Hudson's *Ralph Herne* (1923), a novel, and Morley's *Edmund Burke* (1924). The editions of both are limited, and the publisher's announcements throw a certain glamour of 'fine printing' about the enterprise; but the books themselves, printed in Caslon, have the unassuming and lucid appearance that should be the very first quality of any serious typography. It is to be hoped that this little leaven will have its effect upon the printing of American fiction, most of which has been left so pitiably far behind by the learned presses.

The title-page of *Ralph Herne*, as well as a little book called *The Ballad of William Sycamore* (Brick Row Bookshop, New York, 1923), shows the interest which arabesque flower combinations still have for Mr. Rogers. He has used Garamond only twice in book-work, and seems to consider it unsatisfactory; perhaps it is too dazzling. Garamond capitals, however, were used in an interesting and strikingly successful experiment in printing the hand-book of *The Arts of the Book* exhibition at the Metropolitan Museum in 1924. He had often deplored the overbearing weight of Caslon capitals, and in this instance he substituted those of Monotype Garamont, which gave lightness and more life to the Caslon lower-case without any feeling of incongruity.

Two more books should be mentioned as representing in a striking degree the conviction (if it cannot be called a style) at which Mr. Rogers has perhaps definitely arrived; and a third will possibly give a hint of a new development in his work. The first is a slight Christmas book, Eugene Field's *The Symbol and the Saint* (1924). The title represents a casement window in a nursery, and the whole composition is done in type, cast ornaments being combined with rules, parentheses, commas, other unsuspected printer's equipment and what-not, with the most exquisite ingenuity. The astonishing thing is that it is in good taste, and that the humour is too pretty to be flat. Trickery it is; but the trick succeeds without the aid of an alien line-block or woodcut. This page is

43

only meant to be deft foolery, but there is a line of
ornaments at the top of the first page of text
which in its utter simplicity is a triumph of suggestion: somehow a succession of commas and little leaf-forms holds the image of waves and leap-
ing dolphins as vividly as it is held on the rim of a
Greek vase. Anything as satisfactory and provocative as this preaches its own lesson, which is, in
this case, that typography is a science of symbols,
and that ornament in a book may most fittingly
be restricted to the simple — and therefore inex-
haustible — motives which have a common origin
with types. What rich fields of experiment await
the convert to this belief is shown in the latest
pamphlet for the Monotype Company, in which a
new type face, 'Italian Old Style,' is shown in
combination with bold leaf and flower forms. He
even discovered among some of their *passé* Hal-
lowe'en ornaments a derisively grinning rat and
frog, and the tiny creatures squat among the decorations.

The book has accepted a limitation: the use of
type alone has therefore gained that feckless freedom that can be found only within a limitation.
In some specimen pages at the end another attempt has been made to put all the letters of the
alphabet into a sentence, and in one of them Mr.
Rogers has discarded the well-known text, 'pack

44

my box with five dozen liquor jugs,' in favour of a series of statements about 'xvi brawny gods.' The cover design of a special issue printed privately for Mr. Rogers combines simple, bold curves and rules, such as would be used for display borders, into a pattern suggesting the outline of Italian renaissance shields. In such uses, where there is no attempt to be too explicit in representation, the new manner is undeniably successful and, it may be added, less dangerous in its influence. We shall suffer before long from the laborious inventions of littler men who have seen the originality, but not the discretion, in this *jeu d'esprit*.

There remains one more book which should be singled out for mention for several reasons: *The Portraits of Increase Mather*, privately printed for Mr. William Gwinn Mather in 1924. This book is printed in what has been pronounced an authentic Baskerville type face; but it is not 'period' work. It is the result of independent choice of material; but there is in it nevertheless a rich measure of that quintessential of Mr. Rogers's work —studied sympathy. It is interesting to know that he had been making tentative use of this type in prospectuses and in *The Cemetery at Souain,* a memorial volume printed privately at the Harvard Press in 1921. *The Portraits of Increase Mather*, one of his most recent books, shows that he has perfectly mastered the difficulties of the Baskerville letter, and has managed to throw over its austerity a warmth and naturalness which give it new life and charm. The bobbed descenders of the 'Baskerville' of modern English and American type-founders had prevented his using their versions, but now that a worthy design is at his disposal, it may confidently be expected that his interest in the face, and in the clear bright simplicity of design which he finds suitable for it, will continue. We shall still have from him, doubtless, a succession of such pyrotechnics in type-ornament as the elaborate 'fountain' composed as a title-page for an American paper manufacturer, since his skill in such conjuring is unique.

The very impressiveness of such feats, however, has already led to such imitation as to dull the spur of invention for Mr. Rogers. He has recently expressed a desire to produce editions, in small formats, of only reading matter — books which would be simple and attractive without the self-consciousness implied in that tattered word 'fine.' A series of little books comparable for brilliance and sincerity with the *éditions stéréotypes* of Didot would be a fit problem for the erstwhile 'limited edition man' and a most powerful means of influencing the typographic standards of two continents.

It may be that from an endeavour of this kind there will come a style universal yet still individual. If Mr. Rogers started as a deliberately eclectic and very varied designer, he soon tended towards a certain neo-renaissance style. He borrowed from the Italian fifteenth century and from the French sixteenth century, fusing both into a graceful style which was his characteristic, though not for long. It reached its climax, perhaps, with *The Centaur*. The designer's residence in England marks the beginning of a new tendency in his work, namely the development of the resources of type and cast type-ornaments alone. Now, long before exhausting the opportunities for lively inventions along the lines of *The Pierrot of the Minute*, Mr. Rogers turns to the candour of a transitional type and gives promise of a typography which will be more straightforward and less magnificent than some of his previous work. Yet it will assuredly partake of that curious quality of *amiability*, impossible to analyse and yet so obvious, which may always be seen in his work as an elusive lustre.

TWO CENTURIES OF BOOKS
DESIGNED BY BRUCE ROGERS
AND PRINTED
AT VARIOUS PRESSES

A FOREST HYMN. By William Cullen Bryant. [La Fayette, Ind. c. 1885.]

A single copy, lettered by hand and illustrated with water-color drawings. Small 4to, decorated paper cover. (1)

IMPRESSIONS. A paper read by Mary E. Steele before the Portfolio Club. Indianapolis, 1893.

Title-page drawn by B. R. 4to, paper covers. (2)

HOMEWARD SONGS BY THE WAY. By A. E. [George W. Russell]. Portland, Thomas B. Mosher, 1895.

Old Style type. Decorations by B. R. 925 copies. 16mo, Japan paper covers, uncut. (3)

NOTES: CRITICAL AND BIOGRAPHICAL. By R. B. Gruelle. Collection of W. T. Walters. Indianapolis, 1895.

Old Style Antique type. Initials, headbands, and title-page designed by B. R. 975 copies. Six copies on Whatman paper with initials rubricated. 8vo, limp boards, uncut. (4)

THE BANQUET OF PLATO. Translated by Percy Bysshe Shelley. Chicago, Way and Williams, 1895.

Old Style Antique type. Title-page and decorations by B. R. Square 16mo, cloth, uncut. (5)

PIERRE PUVIS DE CHAVANNES, A SKETCH. By Lily Lewis Rood. Boston, L. Prang & Co. [J. M. Bowles] 1895.

Old Style Antique type. Portrait and reproductions. 500 copies. 8vo, paper covers. (6)

AT THE RIVERSIDE PRESS
Cambridge, Mass.

THE MONUMENT TO ROBERT GOULD SHAW. Its Inception, Completion, and Unveiling. Boston, 1897.

Old Style type. Frontispiece. Title in red and black. 4to, buckram, gilt top. (7)

TUSCAN SONGS. Collected and illustrated by Francesca Alexander. Boston, 1897.

Caslon type. Facsimiles. Title in red and black. Small folio. Two editions, one on Japanese paper in full vellum, gilt. (8)

UNDER THE BEECH-TREE. By Arlo Bates. Boston, 1899.

Old Style type. Initials designed by B. R. Title in red and black. Narrow 8vo, cloth, uncut. (9)

51

A Century of Indian Epigrams. By Paul Elmer More.
Boston, 1899.

Caslon type. 16mo, boards, cloth back, gilt top. (10)

A Little Tour in France. By Henry James. Boston,
1900.

Old Style type. Illustrated by Joseph Pennell. 250 copies on large
paper, 8vo, boards, cloth back, uncut. (11)

Sonnets and Madrigals of Michelangelo Buonarroti.
Rendered into English Verse by W. W. Newell. With
Italian text, Introduction and Notes. [Cambridge]
1900.

Caslon Italic type. Title-page border and decorations. 300 copies
for sale. Two copies on special paper, in parchment binding, with
the decorations painted by B. R. 16mo, cloth, gilt top, uncut. *(12)

Rubáiyát of Omar Khayyám. By Edward Fitzgerald.
Edited by W. A. Brown. [Boston] 1900.

Brimmer type. 300 copies printed in red and black. 8vo, boards,
buckram back, uncut. *(13)

Whittier as a Politician. Edited by S. T. Pickard.
Boston, C. E. Goodspeed, 1900.

Brimmer type. Portrait and facsimile. 150 copies. 8vo, boards,
uncut. *(14)

Log of the Columbia. Season of 1899. By H. C. Leeds.
Cambridge, 1900.

Caslon type. 50 copies printed in red and black for the author. Imperial 8vo, buckram, paper label, uncut. *(15)

Italian Journeys. By W. D. Howells. Boston, 1901.

Old Style type. Illustrations by Joseph Pennell. 300 copies on large
paper. 8vo, boards, cloth back, uncut. (16)

Poems: Now First Collected. By Edmund Clarence
Stedman. Boston, 1901.

Caslon type. Title in red and black. 8vo, buckram, gilt top. (17)

Mater Coronata. Recited at the Bicentennial Celebra-
tion of Yale University xxiii October mdcccci by Edmund Clarence Stedman. Boston, 1901.

Brimmer type. 8vo, decorated boards, cloth back, uncut. *(18)

Of Friendship. An Essay from A Week on the Concord
and Merrimack Rivers. By Henry D. Thoreau. [Cam-
bridge] 1901.

Brimmer type. Woodcut ornament on title. 500 copies. Narrow
12mo, boards, cloth back, uncut. *(19)

VOYAGE AUTOUR DE MA CHAMBRE. Par Xavier de Maistre.
Cambridge, 1901.

Caslon type. Title-page and decorative headings engraved by Sidney
L. Smith. 500 copies. 12mo, boards, parchment back.   *(20)

POEMS. By William Vaughn Moody. Boston, 1901.

Caslon type. 150 copies of first edition. 12mo, bound in boards,
uncut.   (21)

OBERMANN. Selections from Letters to a Friend. By
Etienne Pivert de Senancour. Cambridge, 1901.

Caslon type. Woodcut vignettes on titles. 300 copies. 2 vols. 8vo,
boards, uncut.   *(22)

MR. BROWN'S LETTERS TO A YOUNG MAN ABOUT TOWN.
By W. M. Thackeray. Cambridge, 1901.

Riverside Modern type. 500 copies. 12mo, marbled boards, cloth
back, paper label, uncut.   *(23)

ANNALS OF DE NORMANDIE. Edited by Arthur Sandys.
Cambridge, 1901.

Caslon type. Frontispiece. 50 copies, printed for the Family. 8vo,
boards, buckram back, uncut.   (24)

THE MAY-FLOWER AND HER LOG. Edited by Azel Ames.
Boston, 1901.

Caslon and Original Old Style types. Illustrated. Small 4to, buckram,
uncut.   (25)

DEMOCRACY. By James Russell Lowell. [Cambridge]
1902.

Brimmer type. Woodcut ornament on title. 520 copies. Narrow
12mo, boards, cloth back, uncut.   *(26)

A REPORT OF THE LAST SEA-FIGHT OF THE REVENGE. By
Sir Walter Raleigh. Cambridge, 1902.

Montaigne type, trial fount. With a woodcut after Howard Pyle,
woodcut border and initial. 300 copies, printed by hand. 4to, decorated boards, uncut.   *(27)

THE JOURNAL OF A VOYAGE TO LISBON. By Henry Field-
ing. Cambridge, 1902.

Brimmer type. Portrait. 300 copies. 8vo, boards, buckram back, uncut.   *(28)

THE POEMS OF EDWARD ROWLAND SILL. Cambridge, 1902.

Riverside Modern type. Portrait. 500 copies. Large 8vo, paper
boards, uncut.   (29)

53

JOURNAL OF A TOUR IN THE NETHERLANDS. By Robert Southey. Boston, 1902.

Riverside Modern type. 519 copies. 12mo, marbled paper boards, cloth back, uncut. *(30)

THE ANTI-SLAVERY PAPERS OF JAMES RUSSELL LOWELL. First collected edition. Boston, 1902.

Riverside Modern type. 525 copies. 2 vols. 8vo, paper boards, uncut. (31)

PROTHALAMION : EPITHALAMION. By Edmund Spenser. Boston, 1902.

Brimmer Italic type. Decorations in old red on India paper from drawings by Edwin H. Blashfield. 419 copies. Small folio, boards, uncut. *(32)

THE ESSAYS OF MONTAIGNE. [Translated] by John Florio. Edited, with Bibliography and Notes, by George B. Ives. Boston, 1902–03–04.

Montaigne type. Woodcut portraits, borders and initials. 265 copies. 3 vols. Folio, boards, canvas back, uncut. *(33)

CASTILIAN DAYS. By John Hay. Boston, 1903.

Old Style type. Illustrations by Joseph Pennell. 350 copies on large paper. 8vo, boards, cloth back, uncut. (34)

COMPENSATION. An Essay by Ralph Waldo Emerson. [Boston] 1903.

Brimmer type. Woodcut ornament on title. Printed in red and black. 530 copies. Narrow 12mo, boards, cloth back, uncut. *(35)

INSTRUCTIONS CONCERNING ERECTING OF A LIBRARY. By Gabriel Naudeus. Interpreted by Jo. Evelyn. Cambridge, 1903.

Brimmer type. Printed in red and black. 419 copies. 12mo, boards, leather back, uncut. *(36)

SONGS & SONNETS OF PIERRE DE RONSARD. Selected & Translated into English Verse by Curtis Hidden Page. With an Introductory Essay & Notes. Boston, 1903.

Caslon Italic type. Title border and decorations in red. 425 copies. Narrow 12mo, boards, uncut. *(37)

MY COOKERY BOOKS. By Elizabeth Robins Pennell. Boston, 1903.

Modern type. Reproductions and facsimiles. 330 copies. 4to, marbled boards, buckram back, uncut. *(38)

THE HISTORY OF OLIVER AND ARTHUR. Done into English by William Leighton and Eliza Barrett. [Cambridge] 1903.

Priory Text type. Facsimile woodcuts on title and in the text. Printed in red and black. 330 copies. Small 4to, boards, cloth back, uncut. *(39)

FIFTEEN SONNETS OF PETRARCH. Selected and Translated
by T. W. Higginson. Boston, 1903.

Caslon Italic type. Woodcut title in red and black, text within red
rules. 430 copies. Narrow 12mo, boards, vellum back, uncut. *(40)

PONKAPOG PAPERS. By T. B. Aldrich. Boston, 1903.

Old Style type. 200 copies of the first edition bound in cloth, uncut,
with paper label. Narrow 12mo. (41)

ZUT AND OTHER PARISIANS. By Guy Wetmore Carryl.
Boston, 1903.

Old Style type. Decorative headings. 8vo, cloth, colored top. (42)

KWAIDAN : Stories and Studies of Strange Things. By
Lafcadio Hearn. Boston, 1904.

Old Style type. Printed in red and black. 12mo, cloth, uncut. (43)

THE PARLEMENT OF FOULES. By Geoffrey Chaucer.
[Boston, 1904.]

French Gothic type. Printed in red, blue, and black. Initials
gilded. 325 copies. 8vo, boards, uncut. *(44)

A CHRISTMAS EVE FAMILY STORY. By Charles Dalton.
Boston, 1904.

Brimmer Italic type. 50 copies printed for the author. 8vo, decorated
cloth, uncut. *(45)

A COLLECTION OF THE FACTS AND DOCUMENTS, RELATIVE
TO THE DEATH OF MAJOR-GENERAL ALEXANDER HAMIL-
TON; With Comments . . . By the Editor of the *Evening
Post*. Boston, 1904.

Caslon type. 430 copies. 8vo, cloth, paper label, uncut. (46)

THE OLD MANSE. By Nathaniel Hawthorne. [Boston]
1904.

Brimmer type. Title-page in red and black, with woodcut. 530
copies. Narrow 12mo, boards, cloth back, uncut. *(47)

DOCUMENTS RELATING TO THE PURCHASE AND EXPLORA-
TION OF LOUISIANA. By Thomas Jefferson and William
Dunbar. Boston, 1904.

Caslon type. Portrait and folding map. 550 copies. Royal 8vo,
cloth, paper label, uncut. *(48)

CERTAINE SONETS. By Sir Philip Sidney. [Boston] 1904.

Caslon type. Title-page in black and green. 430 copies. Narrow
12mo, half parchment, uncut. *(49)

GEORGICS OF VIRGIL. Translated . . . by J. W. Mackail.
[Boston, 1904.]

Brimmer Italic type. Decorative illustrations in brown. 330 copies.
Decorated boards, vellum back, uncut. *(50)

LIFE OF DANTE. By Giovanni Boccaccio. Translated by
Philip Henry Wicksteed. [Boston] 1904.

Montaigne type. Woodcut portrait. 265 copies, printed by hand
in red and black. 4to, boards, vellum back, uncut.   *(51)

ENGLISH HOURS. By Henry James. Cambridge, 1905.

Old Style type. Illustrations by Joseph Pennell. 400 copies on large
paper. 8vo, boards, cloth back, uncut.   (52)

THE LIFE AND DEATH OF CARDINAL WOLSEY. By George
Cavendish. Boston and New York, 1905.

Caslon type. Photogravure portraits after Holbein. 1030 copies.
Imperial 8vo, boards, buckram back, uncut.   *(53)

A CONSOLATORIE LETTER OR DISCOURSE. By Plutarch.
Translated by Philemon Holland. [Boston] 1905.

Brimmer type. 375 copies. 8vo, boards, linen back, uncut.   *(54)

SION'S SONETS. Periphras'd by Francis Quarles. Cambridge, 1905.

Brimmer type. Printed in red and black. 430 copies. 16mo, boards,
uncut.   *(55)

THE QUESTION OF OUR SPEECH. THE LESSON OF BALZAC.
Two Lectures by Henry James. Boston, 1905.

Caslon type. Narrow 12mo, boards, cloth back, uncut.   (56)

A SENTIMENTAL JOURNEY THROUGH FRANCE & ITALY.
[By Laurence Sterne.] Boston, 1905.

Brimmer type. Woodcut vignettes on title. 335 copies. 8vo, boards,
buckram back, uncut.   *(57)

THE LOVE POEMS OF JOHN DONNE. Edited by Charles
Eliot Norton. Boston, 1905.

Caslon type. Border on title-page. 535 copies. Narrow 12mo,
boards, vellum back, uncut.   *(58)

THE LIFE AND WORKS OF GEORGE HERBERT. Edited by
G. H. Palmer. Boston, 1905.

Scotch type. 150 copies on large paper. 6 vols. 8vo, boards,
buckram back, uncut.   *(59)

BIBLIOGRAPHY OF NATHANIEL HAWTHORNE. By Nina E.
Browne. Boston, 1905.

Scotch type. 530 copies. Large crown 8vo, cloth, uncut.   (60)

BIBLIOGRAPHY OF NATHANIEL HAWTHORNE. By Wallace
Hugh Cathcart. Cleveland, 1905.

Caslon type. 91 copies for the Rowfant Club. 8vo, boards, uncut. (61)

SAILORS' NARRATIVES OF VOYAGES ALONG THE NEW ENG-
LAND COAST. Edited by G. P. Winship. Boston, 1905.

Caslon type. Maps and facsimiles. 440 copies. 8vo, cloth, uncut. (62)

LETTERS OF MARY BOARDMAN CROWNINSHIELD. Boston,
1905.

Caslon type. 320 copies. 8vo, boards, uncut. (63)

IN MEMORIAM. REBECCA ANDREWS GREENE. [Cam-
bridge, 1906.]

Brimmer type. Portrait. 300 copies privately printed. 8vo, boards,
uncut. (64)

A BIBLIOGRAPHY OF THE WRITINGS OF HENRY JAMES. By
LeRoy Phillips. Boston, 1906.

Caslon type. 250 copies. 8vo, boards, uncut. (65)

BIBLIOGRAPHY OF JAMES RUSSELL LOWELL. By George
Willis Cooke. Boston, 1906.

Scotch type. 530 copies. Large crown 8vo, cloth, uncut. (66)

THE AUTOBIOGRAPHY OF BENJAMIN FRANKLIN. Boston,
1906.

Caslon type. Illustrated. 1030 copies. Imperial 8vo, boards, buckram back, uncut. (67)

PAUL ET VIRGINIE. Par Bernardin de Saint-Pierre. Boston,
1906.

French Didot type. Woodcuts by M. Lamont Brown after copper-
plates in first edition. 250 copies. Imperial 8vo, boards, uncut. *(68)

THEOCRITUS. Translated by C. S. Calverley. Boston, 1906.

Brimmer Italic type. Woodcut decorations. 330 copies. Royal
8vo, decorated boards, uncut. *(69)

A BOOK OF SONGS AND SONNETS. Selected from the Poems
of T. B. Aldrich. Boston, 1906.

Caslon type. Decorated title-page in red and black. 430 copies.
Narrow 12mo, decorated boards, uncut. *(70)

THE SONG OF ROLAND. Translated by Isabel Butler.
[Cambridge, 1906.]

French Gothic and Civilité types. Printed by hand in red, blue,
brown and black. Illustrations colored by hand. 220 copies. Folio,
decorated boards, vellum back, uncut. *(71)

HYDRIOTAPHIA, URNE-BURIALL. By Sir Thomas Browne.
[Cambridge] 1907.

Brimmer type. Woodcut border on title. 385 copies. 4to, crimson
sheepskin, stamped in gold. *(72)

57

ABRAHAM LINCOLN. By Carl Schurz and T. H. Bartlett. Boston, 1907.
Caslon type. Illustrated. 1030 copies. Imperial 8vo, boards, sheepskin back. (73)

SOME UNPUBLISHED CORRESPONDENCE OF DAVID GARRICK. Edited by George Pierce Baker. Boston, 1907.
Oxford type. Portraits. 430 copies. Royal 8vo, buckram, uncut. *(74)

EPISTOLAE HO-ELIANAE. The Familiar Letters of James Howell. With an Introduction by Agnes Repplier. Boston, 1907.
Caslon type. With frontispieces and rubricated titles. 220 copies on large paper. 4 vols. 8vo, boards, cloth back, paper label, uncut. (75)

THE SONNETS OF HENRY WADSWORTH LONGFELLOW. With an Introduction by Ferris Greenslet. Boston, 1907.
Caslon type. Large paper edition of 275 copies. 12mo, boards, paper label, uncut. *(76)

HENRY WADSWORTH LONGFELLOW; a Sketch of his Life. By Charles Eliot Norton. Together with Longfellow's Chief Autobiographical Poems. Boston, 1907.
Caslon type. Two portraits. 400 copies. 8vo, boards, uncut. (77)

THE POEMS OF MARIA LOWELL. Cambridge, 1907.
Monotype Scotch type. Woodcut vignette on title, and frontis-piece portrait. 330 copies. 8vo, boards, uncut. *(78)

EARL PERCY'S DINNER-TABLE. By Harold Murdock. Boston, 1907.
Caslon type. Frontispiece portrait by Sidney L. Smith on India paper. 550 copies. Royal 8vo, cloth, uncut. *(79)

JOHN GREENLEAF WHITTIER. A Sketch of His Life, by Bliss Perry, with Selected Poems. Boston, 1907.
Scotch type. Illustrations. 430 copies. 8vo, cloth, uncut. (80)

AUGUSTUS ST. GAUDENS. By Royal Cortissoz. Boston, 1907.
Montaigne type. Illustrated. 4to, cloth, uncut. (81)

VENETIAN LIFE. By W. D. Howells. Cambridge, 1907.
Old Style type. Illustrations in color by Edmund H. Garrett. 550 copies on large paper. 2 vols. 8vo, boards, uncut. (82)

HORACE WALPOLE, PRINTER. By Percival Merritt. Boston, 1907.
Oxford type. Reproductions. 77 copies printed for the author. 16mo, thin boards, uncut. *(83)

HUMAN BULLETS. A Soldier's Story of Port Arthur. By
Tadayoshi Sakurai. Edited by Alice Mabel Bacon.
Boston, 1907.

Old Style type. Title in red and black. 12mo, decorated cloth, colored
top. (84)

BIBLIOGRAPHY OF OLIVER WENDELL HOLMES. By George
B. Ives. Boston, 1907.

Scotch type. 500 copies. Large crown 8vo, cloth, uncut. (85)

NEW ENGLAND'S PLANTATION. By Rev. Francis Higginson. Salem, 1908.

Caslon type. Woodcut vignette on title-page. 175 copies printed for
the Essex Book and Print Club. Narrow 8vo, boards, cloth back,
uncut. *(86)

THE BANQUET OF PLATO. Translated by Percy Bysshe
Shelley. [Boston] 1908.

Montaigne type. 440 copies. 12mo, boards, uncut. *(87)

PARK-STREET PAPERS. By Bliss Perry. Boston, 1908.

Caslon type. Decorative title and headbands. 250 copies of first
edition, bound in boards, uncut. (88)

THE LIFE AND ADVENTURES OF ROBINSON CRUSOE. By
Daniel Defoe. Boston [1908].

Caslon type. Illustrations after Stothard. Large-paper edition, 4 vols.
8vo, boards, cloth back, uncut. (89)

THE MYSTERY OF GOLF. By Arnold Haultain. Boston,
1908.

Oxford type. Printed in red and black. 440 copies. 12mo, decorated boards, cloth back, uncut. *(90)

BIBLIOGRAPHY OF RALPH WALDO EMERSON. By G. W.
Cooke. Boston, 1908.

Scotch type. 530 copies. Large crown 8vo, cloth, uncut. (91)

BIBLIOGRAPHY OF HENRY DAVID THOREAU. By F. H.
Allen. Boston, 1908.

Scotch type. 530 copies. Large crown 8vo, cloth, uncut. (92)

HINTS FOR LOVERS. By Arnold Haultain. Boston, 1909.

Caslon type. Decorative title and headings in old red. 540 copies.
12mo, boards, paper label, uncut. *(93)

GEOFROY TORY. By Auguste Bernard. Translated by
George B. Ives. [Boston] 1909.

Riverside Caslon type. With reproductions. 370 copies. Imperial
8vo, boards, buckram back, uncut. *(94)

THE ANCESTRY OF ABRAHAM LINCOLN. By J. H. Lea and
J. R. Hutchinson. Boston, 1909.

Caslon type. Title-page in red and black. Illustrated. 1030 copies.
4to, boards, cloth back, uncut. (95)

HAPPY ENDING. [By] Louise Imogen Guiney. Boston, 1909.

Caslon type. Frontispiece. 500 copies on large paper. 8vo, boards,
uncut. (96)

1872 : LETTERS DESCRIBING THE GREAT BOSTON FIRE.
Edited by Harold Murdock. Boston, 1909.

Scotch type. Reproductions of old prints. 500 copies. Large crown
8vo. *(97)

IV SONNETS : WORDSWORTH. [Cambridge] 1909.

Oxford type. Brochure. 143 copies printed by B. R. Square 8vo.
*(98)

THE ADVERTISEMENTS OF THE SPECTATOR. By Lawrence
Lewis. Boston, 1909.

Caslon type. Folding facsimile. 8vo, boards, cloth back, paper label,
uncut. (99)

POEMS. By Winthrop M. Praed. Boston, 1909.

Scotch type. With portrait. 440 copies. 16mo, boards, parchment
back, gilt top, uncut. *(100)

THE COMPLEAT ANGLER. By Izaak Walton. [Cambridge]
1909.

Riverside Caslon type. Vignette on title, with decorative border;
music, and woodcuts of fish. 440 copies. 16mo, boards, paper label,
uncut. *(101)

A POET IN EXILE. Early Letters of John Hay. Edited by
Caroline Ticknor. Boston, 1910.

Oxford type. With portrait and facsimile. 440 copies. 8vo, boards,
paper label, uncut. *(102)

LXXV SONNETS. William Wordsworth. [Cambridge] 1910.

Oxford type. Woodcut on title. 440 copies. Square 8vo, boards,
linen back, uncut. *(103)

BOSTON COMMON. By M. A. DeWolfe Howe. Cambridge,
1910.

Scotch type. Illustrated. 550 copies. Tall 4to, decorated cloth. *(104)

PAN'S PIPES. R. L. S. [Boston] 1910.

Oxford type. Decorations by B. R. 550 copies, 16mo, boards, uncut.
*(105)

RECORDS OF A LIFELONG FRIENDSHIP : R. W. EMERSON
AND W. H. FURNESS. Boston, 1910.

Oxford type. Illustrations. 780 copies. Square 8vo, boards, uncut.
*(106)

KING ARTHUR AND THE TABLE ROUND. With an account
of Arthurian Romance and notes by W. W. Newell.
Boston, 1911.

Old Style type. Titles in red and black. 2 vols. 8vo, half parchment,
gilt tops. (107)

AN EXHIBITION OF PRINTS : MAPS : BROADSIDES : NEWS-
PAPERS : AUTOGRAPHS at The Club of Odd Volumes.
Boston, 1911.

Riverside Caslon type. Pamphlet. 100 copies. 16mo, uncut. *(108)

EXHIBITION OF FIRST EDITIONS OF XVIII CENTURY BOOKS
at The Club of Odd Volumes. Boston, 1911.

Riverside Caslon type. Pamphlet. 100 copies. 16mo, uncut. *(109)

THE CLUB OF ODD VOLUMES. YEAR BOOK FOR 1911.
Boston, 1911. [Reissued 1912.]

Oxford type. Vignette on title. 80 copies. 16mo, boards, paper label,
uncut. *(110)

THE CONSTITUTION OF THE UNITED STATES OF AMERICA
[Boston, 1911.]

Montaigne type. 440 copies. Imperial 8vo, boards, uncut. *(111)

ECCLESIASTES OR THE PREACHER. Boston, 1911.

Riverside Caslon type. Printed in red and black, with Tory borders
on every page. 335 copies. Small 8vo, decorated boards, uncut.
*(112)

NOTES FROM A COUNTRY LIBRARY. By Harold Murdock.
Boston, 1911.

Brimmer Italic type. Vignette illustration. 82 copies printed for The
Club of Odd Volumes. 8vo, decorated boards, cloth back, uncut.
*(113)

MR. WALPOLE'S FRIENDS IN BOSTON. [By John Cotton
Dana.] [Newark] 1911.

Old Style Italic type. 27 copies printed for the author. Brochure.
8vo, uncut. *(114)

LES POINTS DE FRANCE. [By E. Lefébure. Translated by
Margaret Taylor Johnston. New York, The Metropolitan Museum of Art, 1912.]

French Didot type. Illustrations. Brochure. 1000 copies. 8vo. *(115)

61

FRANKLIN AND HIS PRESS AT PASSY. By Luther S. Livingston. New York, The Grolier Club, 1914.

Fry, Brimmer, and Oxford types. With facsimiles. 303 copies (3 on large paper). 8vo, marbled boards, cloth back, uncut. *(116)

MR. RYAN'S COLLECTION. Compiled by Gertrude Barr. New York, 1914.

Oxford type. Frontispiece engraved by Sidney L. Smith. 250 copies printed for Thomas F. Ryan. 16mo, decorated boards, uncut. *(117)

A POLITICAL ROMANCE. By Laurence Sterne. [1759] An Exact Reprint of the First Edition. With an Introduction by Wilbur L. Cross. Boston, 1914.

Caslon and other types. Rubricated title-page. 125 copies printed for The Club of Odd Volumes. 8vo, boards, linen back, paper label, uncut. *(118)

AT THE MUNDER PRESS
Baltimore

A RECORD. [Testimonial to Theodore Marburg. Baltimore, 1912.]

Caslon type. Imperial 8vo. (119)

WILLIAM BYRD, ESQ.: Accounts as Solicitor General of the Colonies . . . and Letters writ to Facetia by Veramour. [New York] 1913.

Caslon type. Hand-ruled. 17 copies printed for Thomas F. Ryan. Royal 8vo, decorated boards, uncut. *(120)

DINNER TO HON. WILLIAM HOWARD TAFT AND DR. WILLIAM HENRY WELCH. Given by Mr. William A. Marburg. Baltimore, 1914.

Bodoni Italic type. With portraits and borders on every page. 70 copies. Brochure. 8vo, decorated boards, uncut. *(121)

AT THE MONTAGUE PRESS
Montague, Mass.

LUTHER S. LIVINGSTON. 1864-1914. [By G. P. Winship] Cambridge, 1915.

Caslon type. With portrait. 200 copies. Privately reprinted from the Papers of the Bibliographical Society of America. 8vo, boards, cloth back, uncut. *(122)

62

An Account of Descriptive Catalogues of Strawberry Hill and of Strawberry Hill Sale Catalogues. Together with a Bibliography. By Percival Merritt. Boston, 1915.

Walpole and Riverside Caslon types. With plates and facsimiles. 75 copies printed for the author. 8vo, marbled boards, linen back, uncut. *(123)

The Centaur. By Maurice de Guérin. Translated by George B. Ives. [Montague] 1915.

Centaur type. With headband and initial. 135 copies privately printed. Tall 4to, boards, uncut. *(124)

AT THE UNIVERSITY PRESS
Cambridge, Mass.

Eleven Examples of Recent Typography by Bruce Rogers. [New York] 1915.

Various types. Separate, in stiff paper covers, from The Printing Art, Dec., 1915. Book and title-pages composed by the Riverside, Montague, Munder, and Museum presses. 4to. (125)

AT THE MALL PRESS
Hammersmith, England

Of the Just Shaping of Letters. By Albrecht Dürer. Translated by R. T. Nichol. New York, 1917.

Centaur type. Decorative title-page and facsimiles. 315 copies on paper and 3 on vellum for The Grolier Club. Small folio, boards, vellum back, uncut. *(126)

AT THE UNIVERSITY PRESS
Cambridge, England

Two Brothers : Accounts Rendered. By Alfred W. Pollard. London, 1917.

Old Style type. Reprint. Brochure. Square 12mo. (127)

The Common Weal. Six Lectures on Political Philosophy. By W. Cunningham. Cambridge, 1917.

Old Style type. 12mo, boards, cloth back, uncut. (128)

On Friendship. 16th century verses. [Cambridge] 1918.

Caslon Italic type. 150 copies privately printed for A. T. Bartholomew and Bruce Rogers. Brochure. 8vo, paper label, uncut. *(129)

STUDIES IN LITERATURE. First Series. By Sir Arthur Quiller-Couch. Cambridge, 1918.

Caslon type. Demy 8vo, cloth, uncut. (130)

MUSICAL ILLUSTRATIONS OF HISTORY AND LITERATURE. By Mr. Edward Dent and Miss Gladys Moger. [London] 1918.

Caslon type. Pamphlet prospectus. 12mo. *(131)

ADDRESS AT THE UNVEILING OF THE ROLL OF HONOUR OF THE CAMBRIDGE TIPPERARY CLUB. 1916. By M. R. James. Cambridge [1918].

Centaur type. Brochure. A small edition in 4to. *(132)

The Same.

Georgian Old Style type. Brochure. 16mo. 1918. *(133)

A COLLECTION OF BOOKS ABOUT CATS. With Notes by Percy L. Babington. Cambridge, 1918.

Georgian Old Style type. Title-page in red and black, with border. 54 copies printed for the editor. 8vo, boards, uncut. *(134)

A JOURNEY TO THE LEVANT IN 1845. By Robert Heywood. Cambridge, 1919.

Monotype Imprint type. With portraits. 100 copies printed for the editor (A. T. Bartholomew). *(135)

HENRY THE SIXTH. By M. R. James. A Reprint of John Blacman's Memoir. Cambridge, 1919.

Caslon type, etc. Demy 8vo. (136)

THE COMMONPLACE BOOK OF ELIZABETH LYTTLETON. By Geoffrey Keynes. Privately printed. Cambridge, 1919.

Caslon type. Brochure. 8vo, uncut. (137)

A DIVINE HEPTALOGY. Compiled by Margaret C. Jenkinson. Privately printed. Cambridge, 1919.

Monotype Imprint type. Square 12mo, paper covers, uncut. *(138)

PICTURE SHOW. By Siegfried Sassoon. [Cambridge] 1919.

Modern type. Border on title. 200 copies printed for the author. Square 8vo, boards, uncut. *(139)

SPARE YOUR GOOD. (London, T. Marshe, ? ab. 1555). Reprinted from the only known copy with an Introduction by E. Gordon Duff. Cambridge, 1919.

Centaur type. Two facsimiles of woodcuts. 250 copies printed. 8vo, stiff paper covers, uncut. *(140)

64

Euclid in Greek. By Sir Thomas L. Heath. Cambridge, 1920.

Monotype Old Style and Greek types. Crown 8vo, cloth, uncut. (141)

The Works of Shakespeare. Edited by Sir Arthur Quiller-Couch and John Dover Wilson. The Tempest. Cambridge, 1921.

Monotype Old Style type. Facsimiles. Fcap. 8vo, cloth, uncut (and leather), gilt top. (142)

AT THE PRINTING HOUSE OF WILLIAM EDWIN RUDGE
Mount Vernon, N. Y.

Twelve Prints by Contemporary American Artists. With an introduction by Carl Zigrosser. New York, 1919.

Garamond type. Preliminary pages for a portfolio of prints. 115 copies for E. Weyhe. Folio. *(143)

Paintings of French Interiors. By Walter Gay. Edited, with an Introduction and Notes, by A. E. Gallatin. New York, 1920.

Garamond type. 50 illustrations. 950 copies. Royal 4to, boards, linen back. (144)

The Journal of Madam Knight. With an Introductory Note by G. P. Winship. Boston, 1920.

Garamond type. Title-page in red and black. Map. 525 copies. 12mo, cloth, uncut. *(145)

A Visit from Saint Nicholas. By Clement C. Moore. Printed as a holiday remembrance by Bruce Rogers and W. E. Rudge. Mount Vernon, 1920.

Original Old Style Italic type. Illustrations by Florence W. Ivins, hand-colored. 8vo, decorated boards, uncut. *(146)

Several Reasons. By Increase Mather. Sentiments on the Small Pox Inoculated. By Cotton Mather. Cleveland, 1921.

Garamond type. Rubricated title. 95 copies privately printed for William Gwinn Mather. 12mo, boards, linen back, uncut. *(147)

The Red Path and The Wounded Bird. By John Freeman. Cambridge, 1921.

Monotype Caslon type. 425 copies (50 on hand-made paper) for Dunster House Bookshop. 8vo, boards, linen back, uncut. *(148)

PRINTING AND THE RENAISSANCE: A Paper Read before the Fortnightly Club of Rochester by John Rothwell Slater. New York, 1921.

Monotype Caslon type. 5 reproductions of printers' marks. 600 copies (100 on hand-made paper). 8vo, boards, uncut.   *(149)

A SELECTION OF BOOKS FROM THE LIBRARY OF THE LATE JOHN WILLIAMS WHITE. Cambridge, 1921.

Garamond, Caslon, and Linotype Greek types. Pamphlet. Printed in red and black. 1000 copies for Dunster House Bookshop. 8vo, uncut.   *(150)

NIGHT AND MOONLIGHT. By Henry D. Thoreau. New York, 1921.

Garamond type. With a woodcut in two colors by Florence W. Ivins. 400 copies (18 on Japanese paper) for Hubert R. Brown. 16mo, boards, uncut.   *(151)

MODERN FINE PRINTING IN AMERICA. An Essay by A. E. Gallatin. New York, 1921.

Garamond type. Small 4to, boards, uncut.   (152)

THE FIFTIETH ANNIVERSARY OF DR. MAX LANDSBERG as Rabbi of Congregation Berith Kodesh. Rochester, N. Y., 1921.

Bodoni type within typographic borders. One copy on vellum and a few on paper. 4to, marbled boards, cloth back, uncut.   *(153)

CONSIDERATIONS ON ENGRAVING. By Timothy Cole. New York, 1921.

Caslon type. Title in red and black. Woodcut by the author. Tall 8vo, boards, uncut.   *(154)

A VISIT FROM ST. NICHOLAS. By Clement C. Moore. Boston, 1921.

Similar to No. 146 but with new woodcuts by Mrs. Ivins printed in colors. 5000 copies for the Atlantic Monthly Press.   (155)

A NOBLE FRAGMENT. Being a Leaf of the Gutenberg Bible. With a Bibliographical Essay by A. Edward Newton. New York, 1921.

Garamond type. Title and introductory pages in red and black to accompany an original leaf of the Bible. 600 copies for Gabriel Wells. 4to.   (156)

PRIAPUS AND THE POOL. By Conrad Aiken. Cambridge, 1922.

Linotype Original Old Style type. 425 copies (50 on hand-made paper signed by the author) for Dunster House Bookshop. Square 8vo, boards, uncut.   *(157)

66

AMERICAN WATER-COLOURISTS. By A. E. Gallatin. New York, 1922.

Bodoni type. 30 reproductions. 950 copies for E. P. Dutton & Co. Imperial 8vo, boards, buckram back, uncut. *(158)

A PROJECT OF UNIVERSAL AND PERPETUAL PEACE. By Pierre-André Gargaz. Reprinted with an English Version by George Simpson Eddy. New York, 1922.

Monotype Caslon type. Rubricated title, decorations and facsimiles. 1250 copies for Mr. Eddy. Narrow 12mo, boards, buckram back, uncut. *(159)

A PLAIN LETTER TO THE LORD CHANCELLOR ON THE INFANT CUSTODY BILL. By the Hon. Mrs. Norton. With an Introductory Note by Frank Altschul. New York, 1922.

Monotype Scotch type. Portrait and facsimile. 150 copies for Mr. Altschul. Royal 8vo, boards, cloth back, paper label, uncut. *(160)

KIDD : A MORAL OPUSCULE. The Verse by Richard J. Walsh. Illustrations by George Illian. New York, 1922.

Goudy New Style type. Illustrations colored by hand. 1000 copies. Square 8vo, glazed boards, uncut. *(161)

THE BRIDE OF HUITZIL. By Hervey Allen. New York, 1922.

Monotype Caslon type. 350 copies in red and black for James F. Drake. 8vo, decorated boards, cloth back, uncut. *(162)

THE RELATION OF ART TO NATURE. By John W. Beatty. New York, 1922.

Linotype Original Old Style type. 950 copies. 8vo, cloth, uncut. *(163)

ABBOTT H. THAYER MEMORIAL EXHIBITION. With an Introduction by Royal Cortissoz. New York, 1922.

Monotype Scotch type. Illustrated. 1000 copies for the Metropolitan Museum of Art. 8vo (a few on large paper). (164)

ETHAN FROME. By Edith Wharton. New York, 1922.

Monotype Caslon type. 2000 copies printed for Charles Scribner's Sons. 8vo, cloth, uncut. (165)

MONOTYPE. Vol. 9, No. 2. [Various Papers on Typography]. Philadelphia, 1922.

Monotype Scotch type, and typographic decorations. Brochure. 20,000 copies for the Monotype Company. 4to. *(166)

ARTHUR RACKHAM. A List of Books Illustrated by Him. Compiled by Frederick Coykendall. With an Introductory Note by Martin Birnbaum. [New York] 1922.

Oxford type. Portrait frontispiece and two reproductions. 175 copies, privately printed. 8vo, boards, uncut. *(167)

JOCELIN OF BRAKELOND. From 'Past and Present.' By Thomas Carlyle. New York, 1923.

Monotype Caslon type. Rubricated title-page. 510 copies. 12mo, cloth, uncut. *(168)

THE PRESBYTERIAN CHILD. [By] Joseph Hergesheimer. New York, 1923.

Monotype Scotch type. 950 copies for Alfred A. Knopf. 8vo, decorated boards, cloth back, uncut. *(169)

THE PIERROT OF THE MINUTE. By Ernest Dowson. New York, 1923.

Deberny type and Fournier vignettes. 300 copies printed in red and black for The Grolier Club. 16mo, boards, uncut *(170)

DREAM CHILDREN. By Charles Lamb. New York, 1923.

Linotype Original Old Style type. Woodcut in colors by Florence W. Ivins. 500 copies printed for Frank Altschul. 8vo, paper. *(171)

RALPH HERNE. By W. H. Hudson. New York, 1923.

Monotype Caslon type and ornaments. 950 copies printed for A. A. Knopf. 8vo, boards, cloth back, uncut. *(172)

MONOTYPE. Vol. 9, No. 6. Private Presses in England, etc. Philadelphia, 1923.

Garamont type, with typographic decorations. Text and rubricated title within ruled margins. Pamphlet. 20,000 copies printed for the Monotype Company. Royal 8vo, uncut. *(173)

THE BALLAD OF WILLIAM SYCAMORE. By Stephen Vincent Benet. New York, 1923.

Original Old Style Italic type, within typographic borders. 400 copies printed for the Brick Row Book Shop. Small 16mo, boards, uncut. *(174)

THE CHRISTMAS DINNER. From "The Sketch Book" by Washington Irving. New York, 1923.

Linotype Original Old Style type. Printed in red and black. 2200 copies. Square 16mo, boards, uncut. *(175)

NEW YEAR'S EVE. By Charles Lamb. New York, 1923.

Monotype Scotch type and decorations. 1000 copies. 8vo, decorated boards, uncut. *(176)

CHRISTMAS EPITHALAMIUM. [By Hervey Allen] N. P. 1923.

Garamond Italic type with decorations in red. 20 copies printed for Mr. and Mrs. W. Van R. Whitall. Square 12mo, wrappers. *(177)

THE CONSTRUCTION OF ROMAN LETTERS. By Albrecht Dürer. Cambridge, 1924.

Printer's note in Centaur type and reproductions within red rules. 350 copies printed for Dunster House Bookshop. 16mo, boards, uncut. *(178)

GEORGE MEREDITH 1909. By J. M. Barrie. New York, 1924.

Garamond type. 500 copies, 16mo, boards, uncut. *(179)

A GUIDE TO AN EXHIBITION OF THE ARTS OF THE BOOK. By W. M. Ivins, Jr. New York, 1924.

Caslon and Garamont types. Illustrations. 1000 copies printed for the Metropolitan Museum of Art. 8vo, paper covers. (180)

EDMUND BURKE. By John Morley. New York, 1924.

Caslon type. 780 copies printed for A. A. Knopf. 8vo, cloth, uncut. (181)

GOLDEN YEARS. A Sonnet Sequence. N. P. 1924.

Caslon type. Fournier ornaments in red. 20 copies, printed privately for William R. Castle, Jr. 16mo, decorated boards, uncut. *(182)

THE SYMBOL AND THE SAINT. By Eugene Field. New York [1924].

Deberny type with typographic decorations. Three small, privately printed editions and 300 copies for sale. 16mo, decorated boards, uncut. *(183)

ITALIAN OLD STYLE. A New Type designed by Frederic W. Goudy. Philadelphia, 1924.

Italian Old Style type and typographic decorations. Pamphlet. 22,500 copies (more or less) printed for the Monotype Company. *(184)

VENETIAN PRINTERS. A Conversation on the Fourth Day of the Bibliographical Decameron of Thomas Frognall Dibdin. [Text of No. 184 with additional notes by W. M. Ivins, Jr., and other alterations.] 1924.

Italian Old Style type and typographic decorations. 223 copies, printed privately for Bruce Rogers. *(185)

MEMORIAL EXHIBITION OF THE WORKS OF JULIAN ALDEN WEIR. With an Introduction by William A. Coffin. New York, 1924.

Monotype Garamont type. Illustrations. Brochure. 1000 copies for the Metropolitan Museum of Art. 8vo. *(186)

69

THE STAR SONG. A Carroll to the King. By R. Herrick. [Mount Vernon] 1924.

Wren Italic type and Fournier ornaments. Text and decorated title within ruled margins in red. 750 copies. 12mo, boards, uncut. *(187)

MEN OF LETTERS OF THE BRITISH ISLES. Portrait Medallions by Theodore Spicer-Simson, with Critical Essays by Stuart P. Sherman. New York, 1924.

Garamont type. 520 copies on Rives and 10 copies on hand-made paper. Imperial 8vo, boards, holland back, uncut. (188)

ORIGINAL MANUSCRIPTS AND DRAWINGS OF ENGLISH AUTHORS. From the Pierpont Morgan Library. On exhibition at the New York Public Library. New York, 1925.

Linotype Original Old Style type. 5000 copies (a few on large paper, in boards) for the Pierpont Morgan Library. 16mo, paper covers. Also a second edition (a few on large paper). *(189)

JOSEPH CONRAD: THE MAN. By Elbridge L. Adams. [and] A BURIAL IN KENT. By John W. Zelie. Together with some Bibliographical Notes. New York, 1925.

Monotype Scotch type, with typographical decorations and frontispiece portrait. 485 copies. 8vo, marbled boards, cloth back, gilt top. *(190)

AT THE HARVARD UNIVERSITY PRESS
Cambridge, Mass.

MEMOIRS OF THE HARVARD DEAD. By M. A. DeWolfe Howe [and others]. Cambridge, 1920–21–22–23–24.

Monotype Scotch type. Portraits. 5 vols. 8vo, cloth, gilt tops. (191)

JOHN WENTWORTH. First Royal Governor of New Hampshire. By Lawrence Mayo. Cambridge, 1921.

Caslon type. Portrait. 500 copies. Small 4to, boards, cloth back, uncut. *(192)

THE CEMETERY AT SOUAIN. Cambridge, 1921.

John Baskerville's type. Illustrations. 100 copies, privately printed. Folio, boards, cloth back, uncut. *(193)

WORDSWORTH IN A NEW LIGHT. By Émile Legouis. Cambridge, 1923.

Monotype Scotch type and decorations. 750 copies (100 on hand-made paper). 8vo, cloth and boards, uncut. *(194)

70

MODERN COLOR. By Carl Gordon Cutler and Stephen C. Pepper. Cambridge, 1923.

Monotype Caslon type. Decorations by W. A. Dwiggins. Square 12mo, decorated boards, colored top. (195)

SONGS AND BALLADS OF THE MAINE LUMBERJACKS. Collected by Roland P. Gray. Cambridge, 1924.

Monotype Caslon type. 8vo, decorated boards, cloth back, colored top. (196)

THE PILGRIMAGE OF ROBERT LANGTON. Transcribed with an Introduction and Notes by E. M. Blackie. Cambridge, 1924.

Monotype Caslon and Black-letter types. Facsimile woodcuts and ornaments. 755 copies. 8vo, boards, linen back, uncut. *(197)

A MOST FRIENDLY FAREWELL TO SIR FRANCIS DRAKE. By Henry Robarts. Transcribed with a short Introduction by E. M. Blackie. Cambridge, 1924.

Caslon, Cloister Italic and Black-letter types. Facsimile woodcuts. 755 copies. 8vo, boards, linen back. *(198)

THE PORTRAITS OF INCREASE MATHER. With some notes on Thomas Johnson, an English Mezzotinter, by Kenneth B. Murdock. Cleveland, 1924.

John Baskerville's type. Colored frontispiece and other portraits 250 copies privately printed for William Gwinn Mather. 4to, marbled boards, morocco back, gilt top. *(199)

PIOZZI MARGINALIA. By Percival Merritt. Cambridge, 1925.

Monotype Scotch type. 750 copies (75 on hand-made paper) 8vo, boards, cloth back, uncut. *(200)

INDEX

ILLUSTRATIONS

Spring Circular

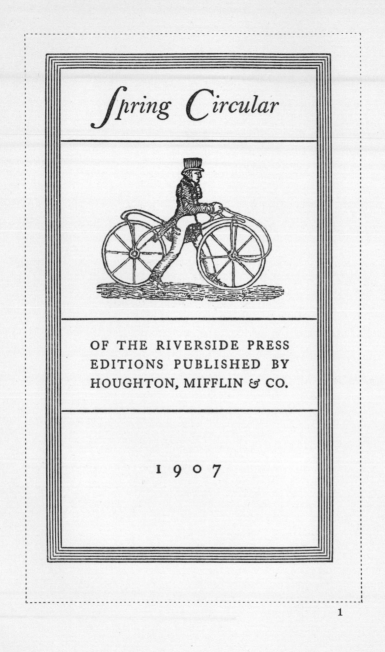

OF THE RIVERSIDE PRESS
EDITIONS PUBLISHED BY
HOUGHTON, MIFFLIN & CO.

1 9 0 7

The Knickerbocker Group

OF

NEW YORK LITERATI

IN these days when New York has become a
metropolitan city, with a population of four
million souls, and the old city has shrunk po-
litically into the borough of Manhattan, it is
not easy to recall the obliterated outlines of the
town which was satirized by the vivacious
young men who wrote the 'Salmagundi Papers.' Unlike Rome, which has been rebuilt

2

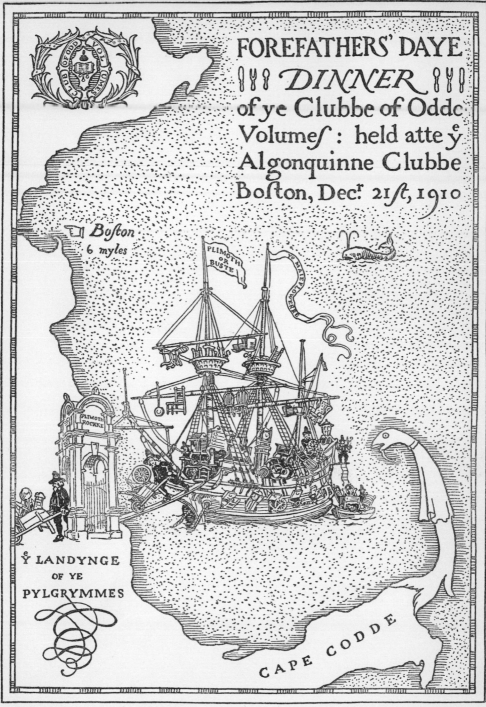

FOREFATHERS' DAYE
DINNER
of ye Clubbe of Odde
Volume∫: held atte ye
Algonquinne Clubbe
Bo∫ton, Dec.r 21∫t, 1910

Bo∫ton
6 myles

PLIMOTH
OR BUSTE

MAYFLOWER

PLIMOTH
ROCKKE

ye LANDYNGE
OF YE
PYLGRYMMES

CAPE CODDE

TO THE RIGHT WORSHIPFUL

JOHN OFFLEY

OF MADELY MANOR IN THE
COUNTY OF STAFFORD, ESQ.
MY MOST HONOURED
FRIEND

SIR,

I Have made so ill use of your former favors, as by them to be encouraged to intreat that they may be enlarged to the patronage and protection of this Book; and I have put on a modest confidence, that I

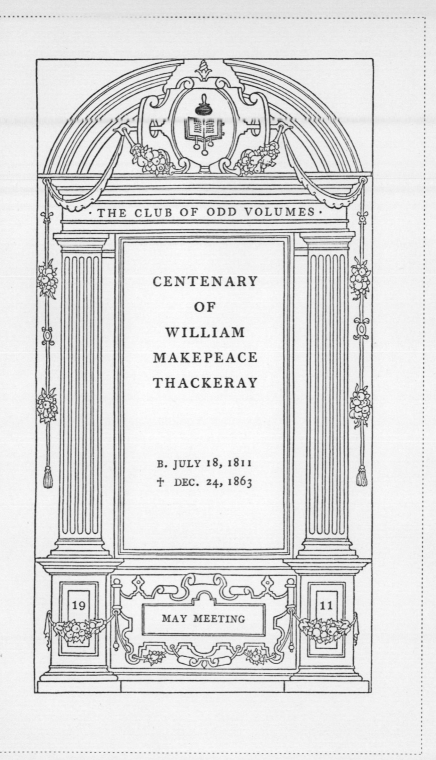

· THE CLUB OF ODD VOLUMES ·

CENTENARY

OF

WILLIAM

MAKEPEACE

THACKERAY

B. JULY 18, 1811
† DEC. 24, 1863

19

11

MAY MEETING

THE world in which we live has
been variously said and sung by
the most ingenious poets and
philosophers: these reducing it
to formulae and chemical ingre-
dients, those striking the lyre in
high-sounding measures for the
handiwork of God. What experience supplies is of a mingled

THE CLUB OF
ODD VOLUMES

℃ Mr. T. Jefferson Coolidge, Jr. invites the members of the Club to visit him at his home at Magnolia on Saturday, June 11, 1910.

℃ Members who can accept will leave the North Terminal Station on the 'Flying Fisherman' at 12.25 P.M. Regular tickets should be purchased and passes for this private train will be provided by Mr. Coolidge through the Clerk pro tem.

℃ Return to Boston will be made on the train leaving Magnolia at 4.15 P.M.

℃ Should the weather be stormy the trip will be postponed to another day. The train conductor will have notice of any postponement.

John Woodbury, Clerk pro tem

NOTES

FROM A COUNTRY LIBRARY

BY

HAROLD MURDOCK

The Executive Committee announces the publication of this volume which has been printed for the Club by Bruce Rogers at The Riverside Press, Cambridge.

This account of a library with its treasures of the eighteenth century, contemporaneous with the old New Hampshire

1

JOSEPH CONRAD : THE MAN

EVER since I came upon "The Nigger of the Narcissus" in tranquil ante-bellum days I had been under the spell of Conrad's art. "Typhoon," "Lord Jim" and "Chance" were read with increasing beguilement, and then "Nostromo," that most astonishing creation of the imagination. One felt that here, indeed, was a magician who could conjure up the very spirit of some Eastern river and make one smell the rank stifling jungle or feel the motion of the ship as it drives before the hurricane. Nothing quite like these stories was to be found in the entire range of English literature. One was prepared to agree with Galsworthy that such writing "is probably the only writing of the last twelve years [he was referring to 1896–1908] that will enrich the English language to any great extent." But what sort of man, one won-

THIS IS THE MONTAIGNE TYPE
cut only in sixteen-point size for the use of
the publishers, Houghton Mifflin Company
at The Riverside Press in Cambridge, Mass.

THIS TYPE IS CALLED 'RIVERSIDE CASLON'
and is a modification of Caslon Old Face. It is cast on
the Monotype at The Riverside Press and employed
at that press for the printing of some of their books.

THIS IS THE TYPE CALLED 'BRIMMER'
a reproduction of a late eighteenth century face
of which the origin is not yet accurately known.
It is transitional in style, like JOHN BASKERVILLE'S.

THIS IS THE BRIMMER ITALIC TYPE
which has been frequently used at The Riverside Press.
When it was reproduced several special swash capitals
were added to it, viz: A D E G M N P & R.

THIS SHOWS THE CENTAUR TYPE
which follows the proportions of Jenson's roman.
It is cast only for The Metropolitan Museum of
Art, New York, and for private use by its designer.

THIS IS JOHN BASKERVILLE'S TYPE
cast from the matrices which are now owned in
Paris, especially for the use of THE HARVARD
UNIVERSITY PRESS, Cambridge, Massachusetts.

THE ITALIC OF BASKERVILLE'S TYPE
is more elegant and characteristic than the roman.
The letters G, J, N, Q, T, Y and Z are unmistakeable.

11

12

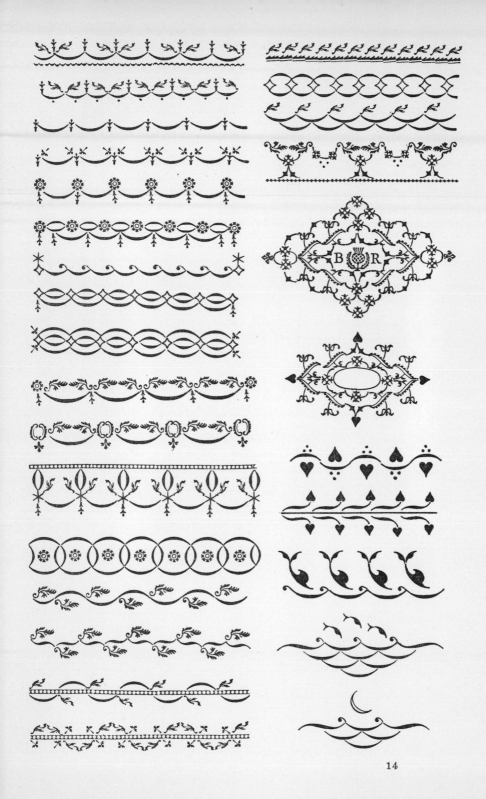

14